# Perl 5
*Pocket Reference*

*Second Edition*

Johan Vromans

*Beijing • Cambridge • Farnham • Köln • Paris • Sebastopol • Taipei • Tokyo*

# *Perl 5 Pocket Reference, Second Edition*

by Johan Vromans

Published by O'Reilly & Associates, Inc., 101 Morris Street, Sebastopol, CA  95472.

**Editors:** Steve Talbott and Gigi Estabrook

**Production Editor:**  Madeleine Newell

**Printing History:**

| February 1996: | First Edition. |
| August 1998: | Second Edition. |

ISBN:  1-56592-495-9

[7/99]

# Table of Contents

# Perl 5
# Pocket Reference

## Introduction

The *Perl 5 Pocket Reference* is a quick reference guide to Larry
Wall's Perl program. It contains a concise description of all
statements, functions, and variables, and lots of other useful
information. It is based on Perl Version 5.005.

The purpose of the Pocket Reference is to aid users of Perl in
finding the syntax of specific functions and statements, and
the meaning of built-in variables. It is *not* a self-contained
user guide; basic knowledge of the Perl language is required.
It is also *not* complete; some of the more obscure variants of
Perl constructs have been left out. But all functions and variables are mentioned in at least one way they can be used.

For more information on Perl, visit the Perl web site at
*http://www.perl.com*.

## Conventions

| | |
|---|---|
| **this** | denotes text that you enter literally. |
| *this* | means variable text, i.e., things you must fill in. |
| *this*† | means that *this* will default to $_ if omitted. |
| word | is a keyword, i.e., a word with a special meaning. |
| RETURN | denotes pressing a keyboard key. |
| [...] | denotes an optional part. |

# Command-Line Options

-a          Turns on autosplit mode when used with -n or -p.
            Splits to @F.

-c          Checks syntax but does not execute. It does run
            **BEGIN** and **END** blocks.

-d[ :*module* ]
            Runs the script under the indicated module. Default
            module is the debugger. Use -de 0 to start the
            debugger without a script.

-D*flags*   Sets debugging flags.

-e *commandline*
            May be used to enter a single line of script. Multiple
            -e commands may be given to build up a multiline
            script.

-F*regex*   Specifies a regular expression to split on if -a is in
            effect.

-h          Prints the Perl usage summary. Does not execute.

-i*ext*     Files processed by the < > construct are to be edited
            in place.

-I*dir*     The directory is prepended to the search path for
            Perl modules, @INC. With -P, also tells the C
            preprocessor where to look for include files.

-l[ *octnum* ]
            (That's the letter ell.) Enables automatic line-end
            processing, e.g., -l013.

-m*module*
            Imports the *module* before executing the script.
            *module* may be followed by an equals sign and a
            comma-separated list of items.

-M*module*
            Same as -m, but with more trickery.

-n          Assumes an input loop around the script. Lines are
            not printed.

| | |
|---|---|
| -p | Assumes an input loop around the script. Lines are printed. |
| -P | Runs the C preprocessor on the script before compilation by Perl. |
| -s | Interprets -**xxx** on the command line as a switch and sets the corresponding variable $**xxx** in the script. |
| -S | Uses the **PATH** environment variable to search for the script. |
| -T | Turns on taint checking. |
| -u | Dumps core after compiling the script. To be used with the *undump*(1) program (where available). Obsoleted. |
| -U | Allows Perl to perform unsafe operations. |
| -v | Prints the version and patch level of your Perl executable. |
| -V[ :*var* ] | Prints Perl configuration information, like -**V:man.dir**. |
| -w | Prints warnings about possible spelling errors and other error-prone constructs in the script. |
| -x[ *dir* ] | Extracts the script from the input stream. If *dir* is specified, Perl switches to this directory before running the script. |
| -0[ *val* ] | (That's the number zero.) Designates an initial value for the record separator $/. See also -l. |

## *Syntax*

Perl is a free-format programming language. This means that in general, it does not matter how a Perl program is written with regard to indentation and lines.

An exception to this rule is when the Perl compiler encounters a sharp or pound symbol (#) in the input: it then discards this symbol and everything following it up to the end of the current input line. This can be used to put comments in Perl programs. Real programmers put lots of useful comments in their programs.

There are places where whitespace does matter: within literal texts, patterns, and formats.

If the Perl compiler encounters the special token __END__, it discards this symbol and stops reading input. Anything following this token is ignored by the Perl compiler, but can be read by the program when it is run.

When Perl is expecting a new statement and encounters a line that starts with =, it skips all input up to and including a line that starts with =cut. This is used to embed program documentation.

## *Embedded Documentation*

Tools exist to extract embedded documentation and generate input suitable for several formatters like troff, LaTeX, and HTML. The following commands can be used to control embedded documentation:

=back    See =over.

=begin *FMT*

      Subsequent text up to a matching =end is only included when processed for formatter *FMT*.

=cut    Ends a document section.

=end *FMT*

      See =begin.

=for *FMT*

      The next paragraph is only included when processed for formatter *FMT*.

**=head1** *heading*

    Produces a first-level heading.

**=head2** *heading*

    Produces a second-level heading.

**=item** *text*

    See **=over**.

**=over** *N*

    Starts an enumeration with indent *N*. Items are specified using **=item**. The enumeration is ended with **=back**.

**=pod**    Introduces a document section. Any of the =-commands can be used to introduce a document section.

These commands apply to the paragraph of text that follows them; paragraphs are terminated by at least one empty line.

An indented paragraph is considered to be verbatim text and will be rendered as such.

Within normal paragraphs, markup sequences can be inserted:

**B**<*text*>  Make text bold (for switches and programs).

**C**<*code*>

    Literal code.

**E**<*escape*>

    A named character, e.g., **E<lt>** means a < and **E<gt>** means a >.

**F**<*file*>  Filename.

**I**<*text*>  Italicize text (for emphasis and variables).

**L**<*name*>

    A cross reference.

**S**<*text*>  Do not break on spaces in *text*.

X<*index*>
　　　　An index entry.

Z<> 　　A zero-width character.

## *Data Types*

Array 　　Indexable list of scalar values

Hash 　　Associative list of scalar values

Scalar 　Strings, numbers, and references

## *Literal Values*

Array 　　(1, 2, 3) is a list of three elements.
　　　　(1, 2, 3)[0] is the first element from this list,
　　　　(1, 2, 3)[-1] the last element.
　　　　( ) is an empty list.
　　　　(1..4) is the same as (1,2,3,4),
　　　　likewise ('a'..'z').
　　　　('a'..'z')[4,7,9] is a slice of a list literal.
　　　　qw/foo bar .../ is the same as ('foo','bar',...).

Array reference
　　　　[1,2,3]

Array reference with named indices (pseudo–hash)
　　　　[{*field1* => *1*, *field2* => *2*, ... }]

Boolean
　　　　Perl has no boolean data type. Anything that is
　　　　undefined or evaluates to the null string, the number
　　　　zero, or the string "0" is considered false, everything
　　　　else is true (including strings like "00"!).

Code reference
　　　　sub { *statements* }

Filehandles
　　　　STDIN, STDOUT, STDERR, ARGV, DATA.
　　　　User-specified: *handle*, $*var*.

Globs     *<pattern>* evaluates to all filenames according to the pattern. Use **<${*var*}>** or **glob** $*var* to glob from a variable.

Hash (associative list)

> (*key1*, *val1*, *key2*, *val2*, …)
> Also (*key1* => *val1*, *key2* => *val2*, …)

Hash reference

> {*key1*, *val1*, *key2*, *val2*, …}

Here–Is     **<<***identifier*

> Shell-style "here document." See the Perl documentation for details.

Numeric

> **123   1_234   123.4   5E-10   0xff** (hex)   **0377** (octal)

Regular Expression

> **qr/***string***/***modifiers*
> See the section "Regular Expressions" for details.

Special tokens

> **__FILE__**: filename; **__LINE__**: line number;
> **__PACKAGE__**: current package;
> **__END__**: end of program; remaining lines can be read using the filehandle **DATA**.

String

> **'abc'**
>
> Literal string, no variable interpolation or escape characters, except \\' and \\\\. Also: **q/abc/**. Almost any pair of delimiters can be used instead of **/.../**.
>
> **"abc"**
>
> Variables are interpolated and escape sequences are processed. Also: **qq/abc/**.
>
> Escape sequences: \\t (Tab), \\n (Newline),
> \\r (Return), \\f (Formfeed), \\b (Backspace),
> \\a (Alarm), \\e (Escape), \\033 (octal), \\x1b (hex),
> \\c[ (control).
>
> \\l and \\u lowercase/uppercase the following character. \\L and \\U lowercase/uppercase until a \\E is

---

*Literal Values*                                            7

encountered. \Q quotes non-word characters until a
\E is encountered.

`command`

Evaluates to the output of the *command*. Also:
qx/*command*/.

## Variables

$var        A simple scalar variable.

$var[27]

28th element of array @var.

$p = \@var

Now $p is a reference to array @var.

$$p[27]

28th element of array referenced by $p.
Also, $p->[27].

$var[-1]

Last element of array @var.

$var[$i][$j]

$j-th element of $i-th element of array @var.

$var{'Feb'}

A value from hash %var.

$p = \%var

Now $p is a reference to hash %var.

$$p{'Feb'}

A value from hash referenced by $p.
Also, $p->{'Feb'}.

$#var       Last index of array @var.

@var        The entire array; in scalar context, the number of
            elements in the array.

@var[3,4,5]

A slice of array @var.

@var{'a','b'}

A slice of %var; same as ($var{'a'},$var{'b'}).

**%var**    The entire hash; in scalar context, true if the hash
          has elements.

**$var{'a',1,...}**
          Emulates a multidimensional list (deprecated).

**$c = \&mysub**
          Now **$c** is a reference to subroutine **mysub**.

**$c->( *args* )**
          Calls the subroutine via the reference.

*pkg*::*var*  A variable from a package, e.g., **$pkg::var**, **@pkg::ary**.

\\*thingie*  Reference to a thingie, e.g., **\$var**, **\%hash**.

\**name*    Refers to all thingies represented by *name*.
          **\*n1 = \*n2** makes all **n1** aliases for **n2**.
          **\*n1 = \$n2** makes the package variable **$n1** an alias
          for **$n2**.

You can always use a *block* (see the section "Statements")
returning the right type of reference instead of the variable
identifier, e.g., **${...}**, **&{...}**. **$$p** is just a shorthand for **${$p}**.

## *Context*

Boolean
          A special form of scalar context in which it only
          matters if the result is true or false.

List      A list value or an array is expected.

Scalar    A single scalar value is expected.

Void      No value is expected. If a value is provided, it is
          discarded.

The following functions relate to context:

**scalar** *expr*

          Forces scalar context for the expression.

**wantarray**

          Returns true if the current context expects a list
          value, undef in void context.

---

# Operators and Precedence

Perl operators have the following associativity and precedence, listed from highest precedence to lowest.

| Assoc. | Operators | Description |
|---|---|---|
| left | terms and list operators | See below. |
| left | -> | Infix dereference operator. |
| | ++ <br> -- | Auto-increment (magical on strings). <br> Auto-decrement. |
| right | ** | Exponentiation. |
| right <br> right <br> right | \ <br> ! ~ <br> + - | Reference to an object (unary). <br> Unary negation, bitwise complement. <br> Unary plus, minus. |
| left <br><br> left | =~ <br><br> !~ | Binds a scalar expression to a pattern match. <br> Same, but negates the result. |
| left | * / % x | Multiplication, division, modulo, repetition. |
| left | + - . | Addition, subtraction, concatenation. |
| left | >> << | Bitwise shift right, bitwise shift left. |
| | named unary operators | e.g., sin, chdir, -f, -M. |
| | < > <= >= <br> lt gt le ge | Numerical relational operators. <br> String relational operators. |
| | == != <=> <br> eq ne cmp | Numerical equal, not equal, compare. <br> Stringwise equal, not equal, compare. <br> Compare operators return -1 (less), <br> 0 (equal), or 1 (greater). |
| left | & | Bitwise AND. |
| left | \| ^ | Bitwise OR, exclusive OR. |
| left | && | Logical AND. |
| left | \|\| | Logical OR. |
| | .. <br><br> ... | In scalar context, range operator. <br> In list context, enumeration. <br> Alternative range operator. |
| right | ?: | Conditional (if ? then : else) operator. |

| Assoc. | Operators | Description |
|--------|-----------|-------------|
| right | `=` `+=` `-=` etc. | Assignment operators. |
| left | `,` | Comma operator, also list element separator. |
| left | `=>` | Same, enforces the left operand to be a string. |
| | list operators (rightward) | See below. |
| right | **not** | Low precedence logical NOT. |
| left | **and** | Low precedence logical AND. |
| left | **or** **xor** | Low precedence logical OR, exclusive OR. |

Parentheses can be used to group an expression into a term.

A list consists of expressions, variables, or lists, separated by commas. An array variable or an array slice may always be used instead of (or as part of) a list.

Perl functions that can be used as list operators have either very high or very low precedence, depending on whether you look at the left side of the operator or at the right side of the operator. Parentheses can be added around the parameter lists to avoid precedence problems.

The logical operators do not evaluate the right operand if the result is already known after evaluation of the left operand.

## Statements

A statement is an expression, optionally followed by a modifier, and terminated with a semicolon. Statements can be combined to form a *block* when enclosed in {}. The semicolon may be omitted after the last statement of the *block*.

Execution of expressions can depend on other expressions using one of the modifiers if, unless, for, foreach, while, or until, e.g.:

```
expr1 if expr2;
expr1 foreach list;
expr1 until expr2;
```

The logical operators | |, &&, or ?: also allow conditional execution:

```
expr1 | | expr2;
expr1 ? expr2 : expr3;
```

*blocks* may be used to control flow:

if ( *expr* ) *block* [ [ elsif ( *expr* ) *block* ... ] else *block* ]

unless ( *expr* ) *block* [ else *block* ]

[ *label*: ] while ( *expr* ) *block* [ continue *block* ]

[ *label*: ] until ( *expr* ) *block* [ continue *block* ]

[ *label*: ] for ( [ *expr* ] ; [ *expr* ] ; [ *expr* ] ) *block*

[ *label*: ] foreach *var*† ( *list* ) *block*

[ *label*: ] *block* [ continue *block* ]

for and foreach can be used interchangeably.

Program flow can be controlled with:

goto *label*

> Finds the statement labeled with *label* and resumes execution there. *label* may be an expression that evaluates to the name of a label.

last [ *label* ]

> Immediately exits the loop in question. Skips the continue block.

---

next [ *label* ]

> Executes the **continue** block and starts the next iteration of the loop.

redo [ *label* ]

> Restarts the loop block without evaluating the conditional again. Skips the **continue** block.

Special forms are:

> do *block* while *expr* ;
> do *block* until *expr* ;

which are guaranteed to perform *block* once before testing *expr*, and

> do *block*

which effectively turns *block* into an expression.

## Subroutines, Packages, and Modules

&*subroutine list*

> Executes a *subroutine* declared by a **sub** declaration, and returns the value of the last expression evaluated in *subroutine. subroutine* can be an expression yielding a reference to a code object. The **&** may be omitted if the subroutine has been declared before being used, or the *list* is parenthesized.

bless *ref* [ , *classname* ]

> Turns the object *ref* into an object in *classname*. Returns the reference.

caller [ *expr* ]

> Returns a list ($package, $file, $line, ...) for a specific subroutine call. **caller** returns this information for the current subroutine, **caller(1)** for the caller of this subroutine, etc. Returns **false** if no caller.

---

do *subroutine* *list*
> Deprecated form of &*subroutine*.

goto &*subroutine*
> Substitutes a call to *subroutine* for the current subroutine.

import *module* [ [ *version* ] *list* ]
> Imports the named items from *module*.

no *module* [ *list* ]
> Cancels imported semantics. See use.

package [ *namespace* ]
> Designates the remainder of the current block as a package with a namespace, or without one if *namespace* is omitted.

prototype *function*
> Returns the prototype of the function as a string, or undef if the function has no prototype.

require *expr*†
> If *expr* is numeric, requires Perl to be at least that version. Otherwise *expr* must be the name of a file that is included from the Perl library. Does not include more than once, and yields a fatal error if the file does not evaluate to a true value. If *expr* is a bare word, assumes extension .**pm** for the name of the file. This form of module loading does not risk altering your namespace.

return [ *expr* ]
> Returns from a subroutine with the value specified; if no value, returns undef in scalar context and an empty list in list context.

sub [ *name* ] [ ( *proto* ) ] *block*
> Designates *name* as a subroutine. Parameters are passed by reference as array @_. Returns the value of the last expression evaluated. *proto* can be used to define the required parameters. Without a *block* it is just a forward declaration, without the *name* it is an anonymous subroutine.

[ sub ] **BEGIN** *block*

> Defines a setup *block* to be called before execution.

[ sub ] **END** *block*

> Defines a cleanup *block* to be called upon termination.

[ sub ] **INIT** *block*

> Defines an initialization *block* to be called after compilation, just before execution.

use *module* [ [ *version* ] *list* ]

> Loads the named module into the current package at compile time.

# Object-Oriented Programming

Perl rules of object-oriented programming are as follows:

- An object is simply a reference that happens to know which class it belongs to. Objects are blessed, references are not.

- A class is simply a package that happens to provide methods to deal with object references. If a package fails to provide a method, the base classes as listed in **@ISA** are searched.

- A method is simply a subroutine that expects an object reference (or a package name, for static methods) as the first argument.

  Methods can be called with:

  > *objref –> method parameters*     or
  > *method objref parameters*

## Standard Methods

The package **UNIVERSAL** contains methods that are automatically inherited by all other classes:

can *method*

> Returns a reference to the method if its object has it, undef otherwise.

isa *class*

> Returns true if its object is blessed into a subclass of *class*.

VERSION [ *need* ]

> Returns the version of the class. Checks the version if *need* is supplied.

## Pragmatic Modules

Pragmatic modules affect the compilation of your program. Pragmatic modules can be activated (imported) with use and deactivated with no. These are usually block scoped.

attrs *attributes*

> Sets/gets attributes of a subroutine.
>
> **use attrs "method"** indicates that the invoking subroutine is a method.
>
> **use attrs "locked"** protects the invoking subroutine against concurrent access.

autouse *mods*

> Each of the named modules will not be loaded until one of its functions is called.

base *classes*

> Establishes an IS-A relationship with the base classes at compile time.

blib [ *dir* ]

> Uses MakeMaker's uninstalled version of a package. *dir* defaults to the current directory.

**constant** *name* => *value*
> Pragma to declare constants.

**diagnostics** [ **-verbose** ]
> Forces verbose warning diagnostics and suppress
> duplicate warnings.

**fields** *names*
> Implements compile-time class fields using pseudo-
> hashes.

**integer**   Computes arithmetic in integer instead of double
> precision.

**less** *what*
> Requests less of something from the compiler
> (unimplemented).

**lib** *names*
> Adds libraries to **@INC**, or remove them.

**locale**   Uses and avoids POSIX locales for built-in opera-
> tions.

**ops** *operations*
> Restricts unsafe operations when compiling.

**overload** *operator* => *subref*
> Packages for overloading Perl operators. *operator* is
> the operator (as a string), *subref* a reference to the
> subroutine handling the overloaded operator.
> Example: **use overload "+" => \&my_add;**

**re** *behaviors*
> Alters regular expression behavior.
> **use re "eval"** allows zero-width code evaluation
> assertions (see the section "Regular Expressions").
> **use re "taint"** propagates tainting.

**sigtrap** *info*
> Enables simple signal handling.
> Example: **use sigtrap qw(SEGV TRAP);**

---

**strict** [ *constructs* ]

> Restricts unsafe constructs.
>
> **use strict "refs"** restricts the use of symbolic references.
>
> **use strict "vars"** requires all variables to be either my or fully qualified.
>
> **use strict "subs"** restricts the use of bareword identifiers that are not subroutines.
>
> Without *constructs*, affects all of them.

**subs** *names*

> Predeclares subroutine names, allowing you to use them without parentheses even before they are declared.
>
> Example: **use subs qw(ding dong);**

**vars** *names*

> Predeclares variable names, allowing you to use them under the strict pragma.
>
> Example: **use vars qw($foo @bar);**

**vmsish** [ *features* ]

> Controls VMS-specific language features. VMS only.
>
> **use vmsish "exit"** enables VMS-style exit codes.
>
> **use vmsish "status"** allows system commands to deliver VMS-style exit codes to the calling program.
>
> **use vmsish "time"** makes all times relative to the local time zone.
>
> Without *features*, affects all of them.

## *Arithmetic Functions*

| | |
|---|---|
| abs *expr*† | Returns the absolute value of its operand. |
| atan2 *y*, *x* | Returns the arctangent of $y/x$ in the range $-\pi$ to $\pi$. |
| cos *expr*† | Returns the cosine of *expr* (expressed in radians). |
| exp *expr*† | Returns *e* to the power of *expr*. |
| int *expr*† | Returns the integer portion of *expr*. |

log *expr*†    Returns the natural logarithm (base *e*) of *expr*.

rand [ *expr* ]

> Returns a random fractional number between 0 (inclusive) and the value of *expr* (exclusive). If *expr* is omitted, defaults to 1.

sin *expr*†    Returns the sine of *expr* (expressed in radians).

sqrt *expr*†    Returns the square root of *expr*.

srand [ *expr* ]

> Sets the random number seed for the rand operator.

time    Returns the number of non-leap seconds since whatever time the system considers to be the epoch. Suitable for feeding to gmtime and localtime.

## *Conversion Functions*

chr *expr*†

> Returns the character represented by the decimal value *expr*.

gmtime [ *expr* ]

> In list context, converts a time as returned by the time function to a 9-element list (0:$sec, 1:$min, 2:$hour, 3:$mday, 4:$mon, 5:$year, 6:$wday, 7:$yday, 8:$isdst) with the time localized for the standard Greenwich time zone.
>
> In scalar context, converts it to print format. $mon has the range 0 (January) .. 11 (December) and $wday has the range 0 (Sunday) .. 6 (Saturday). *expr* defaults to the current time.

hex *expr*†

> Returns the decimal value of *expr* interpreted as a hex string.

localtime [ *expr* ]

> Like gmtime, but with the time localized for the local time zone.

---

oct *expr*†

> Returns the decimal value of *expr* interpreted as an octal string. If *expr* starts off with 0x, interprets it as a hex string instead.

ord *expr*†

> Returns the ASCII value of the first character of *expr*.

vec *expr, offset, bits*

> Treats string *expr* as a vector of unsigned integers of *bits* bits each, and yields the decimal value of the element at *offset*. *bits* must be a power of 2 between 1 and 32. May be assigned to.

## *Structure Conversion*

pack *template, list*

> Packs the values in *list* into a binary structure using *template*. Returns a string containing the structure.

unpack *template, expr*

> Unpacks the structure *expr* into a list, using *template*.

*template* is a sequence of characters as follows:

| a | / | A | ASCII string, null- / space-padded |
|---|---|---|---|
| b | / | B | Bit string in ascending / descending order |
| c | / | C | Signed / unsigned char value |
| f | / | d | Single / double float in native format |
| h | / | H | Hex string, low / high nybble first |
| i | / | I | Signed / unsigned integer value |
| l | / | L | Signed / unsigned long value |
| n | / | N | Short / long in network (big endian) byte order |
| s | / | S | Signed / unsigned short value |
| u | / | p | Uuencoded string / pointer to a string |
| P | | | Pointer to a structure (fixed-length string) |
| v | / | V | Short / long in VAX (little endian) byte order |
| w | | | A BER compressed integer |
| x | / | @ | Null byte / null fill until position |
| X | | | Back up a byte |

Each character may be followed by a decimal number that will be used as a repeat count; an asterisk (*) specifies all remaining arguments. If the format is preceded with %*n*, **unpack** returns an *n*-bit checksum instead. *n* defaults to 16. Whitespace may be included in the template for readability.

## *String Functions*

chomp *list*†

> Removes line endings from all elements of the list; returns the (total) number of characters removed.

chop *list*†

> Chops off the last character on all elements of the list; returns the last chopped character.

crypt *plaintext, salt*

> Encrypts a string (irreversibly).

eval *expr*†

> *expr* is parsed and executed as if it were a Perl program. The value returned is the value of the last expression evaluated. If there is a syntax error or runtime error, **undef** is returned by **eval**, and $@ is set to the error message. See also **eval** in the section "Miscellaneous."

index *str, substr* [ , *offset* [ , *replacement* ] ]

> Returns the position of *substr* in *str* at or after *offset*. Replaces the found substring by the replacement text if specified. If the substring is not found, returns -1.

lc *expr*† Returns a lowercase version of *expr*.

lcfirst *expr*†

> Returns *expr* with its first character in lowercase.

length *expr*†

> Returns the length in bytes of *expr*.

quotemeta *expr*†

> Returns *expr* with all regular expression metacharacters quoted.

---

rindex *str*, *substr* [ , *offset* ]

> Returns the position of the last *substr* in *str* at or before *offset*.

substr *expr*, *offset* [ , *len* ]

> Extracts a substring of length *len* starting at *offset* out of *expr* and returns it. If *offset* is negative, counts from the end of the string. If *len* is negative, leaves that many characters off the end of the string. May be assigned to.

uc *expr*†

> Returns an uppercase version of *expr*.

ucfirst *expr*†

> Returns *expr* with its first character in uppercase.

## *Array and Hash Functions*

delete $*hash*{*key*}

delete @*hash*{*key1*, *key2*, ...}

> Deletes the specified value(s) from the specified hash. Returns the deleted value(s) (unless *hash* is tied to a package that does not support this).

each %*hash*

> Returns a 2-element list consisting of the key and value for the next value of the hash. Entries are returned in an apparently random order. After all values of the hash have been returned, an empty list is returned. The next call to **each** after that will start iterating again.
>
> A call to **keys** or **values** will reset the iteration.

exists *expr*

> Checks if the specified hash key exists in this hash.

grep *expr*, *list*

grep *block list*

> Evaluates *expr* or *block* for each element of the *list*, locally setting **$_** to refer to the element. Modifying **$_** will modify the corresponding element from *list*.

In list context, returns the list of elements from *list* for which *expr* returned true. In scalar context, returns the number of such elements.

join *expr, list*

Joins the separate strings of *list* into a single string with fields separated by the value of *expr,* and returns the string.

keys %*hash*

In list context, returns a list of all the keys of the named hash. In scalar context, returns the number of elements of the hash.

map *expr, list*

map *block list*

Evaluates *expr* or *block* for each element of the *list,* locally setting $_ to refer to the element. Modifying $_ will modify the corresponding element from *list.* Returns the list of results.

pop [ @*array* ]

Pops off and returns the last value of the array. If @*array* is omitted, pops **@ARGV** or @_ depending on the current lexical scope.

push @*array, list*

Pushes the values of the *list* onto the end of the array. Returns the new length of the array.

reverse *list*

In list context, returns the *list* in reverse order. In scalar context, concatenates the list elements and returns the reverse of the resulting string.

scalar @*array*

Returns the number of elements in the array.

scalar %*hash*

Returns a true value if the hash has elements defined.

**shift** [ *@array* ]

> Shifts the first value of the array off and returns it, shortening the array by 1 and moving everything down. If *@array* is omitted, shifts **@ARGV** or **@_** depending on the current lexical scope.

**sort** [ *subroutine* ] *list*

> Sorts the *list* and returns the sorted list value. *subroutine*, if specified, must return less than zero, zero, or greater than zero, depending on how the elements of the list (available to the routine as package global variables **$a** and **$b**) are to be ordered. *subroutine* may be (a variable containing) the name of a user-defined routine, or a *block*.

**splice** *@array*, *offset* [, *length* [ , *list* ] ]

> Removes the elements of *@array* designated by *offset* and *length*, and replaces them with *list* (if specified). Returns the elements removed. If *offset* is negative, counts from the end of the array.

**split** [ *pattern* [ , *expr* [ , *limit* ] ] ]

> Splits *expr* (a string) into a list of strings, and returns it. If *limit* is specified, splits into at most that number of fields. If *pattern* is omitted, splits at the whitespace (after skipping any leading whitespace). If not in list context, returns the number of fields and splits to @_. See also the section "Search and Replace Functions."

**unshift** *@array*, *list*

> Prepends *list* to the front of the array, and returns the number of elements in the new array.

**values** *%hash*

> Returns a list consisting of all the values of the named hash.

## Regular Expressions

Each character matches itself, unless it is one of the special characters + ? . * ^ $ ( ) [ ] { } | \. The special meaning of these characters can be escaped using a \.

.           Matches an arbitrary character, but not a newline unless the **s** modifier is used (see **m/ /s** in section "Search and Replace Functions").

(...)        Groups a series of pattern elements to a single element.

^           Matches the beginning of the target. In multiline mode (see **m//m** in section "Search and Replace Functions") also matches after every newline character.

$           Matches the end of the line, or before a final newline character. In multiline mode also matches before every newline character.

[ ... ]      Denotes a class of characters to match. [^...] negates the class.

(... | ... | ...)
            Matches one of the alternatives.

(?# *text*)
            Comment.

(?: *regex*)
            Like (*regex*) but does not make back-references. Modifiers may be placed between the ? and : (see ? *modifier*, later in this list).

(?= *regex*)
            Zero-width positive look-ahead assertion.

(?! *regex*)
            Zero-width negative look-ahead assertion.

(?< *regex*)
            Zero-width positive look-behind assertion.

(?<! *regex*)
            Zero-width negative look-behind assertion.

---

**(?{ code })**

> Executes Perl code while matching. Always succeeds with zero width.
>
> Requires the **re "eval"** pragma.

**(?> regex)**

> Anchored subpattern.

**(?(cond)ptrue [ | pfalse ] )**

> Selects a pattern depending on the condition. *cond* should be the number of a parenthesised subpattern, or one of the zero-width look-ahead, look-behind and evaluate assertions.

**(? modifier)**

> Embedded pattern-match modifier. *modifier* can be one or more of i, m, s, or x. Modifiers can be switched off by preceding the letter(s) with a minus sign.

Quantified subpatterns match as many times as possible. When followed with a ? they match the minimum number of times. These are the quantifiers:

**+**       Matches the preceding pattern element one or more times.

**?**       Matches zero or one times.

**\***       Matches zero or more times.

**{n,m}**    Denotes the minimum *n* and maximum *m* match count. {*n*} means exactly *n* times; {*n*,} means at least *n* times.

A \ escapes any special meaning of the following character if non-alphanumeric, but it turns most alphanumeric characters into something special:

**\w**      Matches alphanumeric, including _, **\W** matches non-alphanumeric.

**\s**      Matches whitespace, **\S** matches non-whitespace.

**\d**      Matches digits, **\D** matches non-digits.

| \A | Matches the beginning of the string. |
|---|---|
| \Z | Matches the end of the string, or before a newline at the end. |
| \z | Matches the end of the string. |
| \b | Matches word boundaries, \B matches non-boundaries. |
| \G | Matches where the previous m//g search left off. |

\t, \n, \r, \f, \a, \e, \0*XX*, \x*XX*, \c*X*, \l, \u, \L, \U, \E and \Q have their usual meaning, see "String" in the section "Literal Values."

\w, \W, \s, \S, \d, and \D
These may be used within character classes, but \b denotes a backspace in this context.

Back-references:

| \1...\9 | Refer to matched subexpressions, grouped with ( ), inside the match. |
|---|---|
| \10 and up | Can also be used if the pattern matches that many subexpressions. |

See also $1...$9, $+, $&, $\`, and $' in the section "Special Variables."

With modifier x, whitespace and comments can be used in the patterns for readability purposes.

## *Search and Replace Functions*

If the right hand side of the =~ or !~ is an expression rather than a search pattern, substitution, or transliteration, it is interpreted as a search pattern at runtime.

[ *expr* =~ ] [ m ] */pattern/* [ g [ c ] ] [ i ] [ m ] [ o ] [ s ] [ x ]
Searches *expr* (default: $_) for a pattern.
If you prepend an m you can use almost any pair of delimiters instead of the slashes.

For =~, its negation !~ may be used, which is true when =~ would return a false result.

If used in list context, a list is returned consisting of the subexpressions matched by the parentheses in the pattern, i.e., **($1, $2, $3,...)**.

Optional modifiers: c prepares for continuation; g matches as many times as possible; i searches in a case-insensitive manner; o interpolates variables only once. m treats the string as multiple lines; s treats the string as a single line; x allows for regular expression extensions.

If *pattern* is empty, the most recent pattern from a previous successful match or replacement is used.

With g, the match can be used as an iterator in scalar context.

*?pattern?*

This is just like the */pattern/* search, except that it matches only once between calls to the reset operator.

[ *$var* =~ ] s/*pattern*/*newtext*/ [ e ] [ g ] [ i ] [ m ] [ o ] [ s ] [ x ]

Searches the string *var* (default $_) for a pattern, and if found, replaces that part with the replacement text. It returns the number of substitutions made, if any; if no substitutions are made, it returns false.

Optional modifiers: g replaces all occurrences of the pattern; e evaluates the replacement string as a Perl expression; for the other modifiers, see */pattern/* matching.

Almost any delimiter may replace the slashes; if single quotes are used, no interpolation is done on strings between the delimiters. Otherwise, strings are interpolated as if in double quotes.

If bracketing delimiters are used, *pattern* and *newtext* may have their own delimiters, e.g., s(foo)[bar]

If *pattern* is empty, the most recent pattern from a previous successful match or replacement is used.

[ $*var* =~ ] tr/*searchlist*/*replacementlist*/ [ c ] [ d ] [ s ]

Transliterates all occurrences of the characters found in the search list into the corresponding character in the replacement list. It returns the number of characters replaced. y may be used instead of tr.

Optional modifiers: c complements the *searchlist*; d deletes all characters found in *searchlist* that do not have a corresponding character in *replacementlist*; s squeezes all sequences of characters that are translated into the same target character into one occurrence of this character.

pos *scalar*†

Returns the position where the last m//g search left off for *scalar*. May be assigned to.

qr/*string*/*modifiers*

Compiles the string as a pattern and returns the compiled pattern as a scalar value.

study $*var*†

Studies the scalar variable $*var* in anticipation of performing many pattern matches on its contents before the variable is next modified.

## *File Test Operators*

These unary operators take one argument, either a filename or a filehandle, and test the associated file to see if something is true about it. If the argument is omitted, they test $_ (except for -t, which tests **STDIN**). If the special argument _ (underscore) is passed, they use the information from the preceding test or stat call.

-r -w -x

File is readable/writable/executable by effective uid/gid.

**-R -W -X**
> File is readable/writable/executable by real uid/gid.

**-o -O**  File is owned by effective/real uid.

**-e -z**  File exists/has zero size.

**-s**  File exists and has non-zero size. Returns the size.

**-f -d**  File is a plain file/a directory.

**-l -S -p**
> File is a symbolic link/a socket/a named pipe
> (FIFO).

**-b -c**  File is a block/character special file.

**-u -g -k**
> File has setuid/setgid/sticky bit set.

**-t**  Tests if filehandle (**STDIN** by default) is opened to a
> tty.

**-T -B**  File is a text/non-text (binary) file. **-T** and **-B** return
> true on a null file, or a file at EOF when testing a
> filehandle.

**-M -A -C**
> File modification/access/inode-change time. Mea-
> sured in days. Value returned reflects the file age at
> the time the script started. See also **$^T** in the sec-
> tion "Special Variables."

## File Operations

Functions operating on a list of files return the number of
files successfully operated upon.

chmod *list*
> Changes the permissions of a list of files. The first
> element of the list must be the numerical mode in
> octal, e.g., 0644.

chown *list*
> Changes the owner and group of a list of files. The
> first two elements of the list must be the numerical
> uid and gid. If gid is −1, the group is not changed.

**link** *oldfile, newfile*

>Creates a new filename linked to the old filename.

**lstat** *file*  Like stat, but if the last component of the filename is a symbolic link, **stat**s the link instead of the file it links to.

**mkdir** *dir, perm*

>Creates a directory with given permissions, e.g., 0755.

**readlink** *expr†*

>Returns the value of a symbolic link.

**rename** *oldname, newname*

>Changes the name of a file.

**rmdir** *filename†*

>Deletes the directory if it is empty.

**stat** *file*  Returns a 13-element list (0:$dev, 1:$ino, 2:$mode, 3:$nlink, 4:$uid, 5:$gid, 6:$rdev, 7:$size, 8:$atime, 9:$mtime, 10:$ctime, 11:$blksize, 12:$blocks). *file* can be a filehandle, an expression evaluating to a filename, or _ to refer to the last file test operation or stat call. Returns an empty list if the **stat** fails.

>Use the standard module **File::stat** for easy access to this information.

**symlink** *oldfile, newfile*

>Creates a new filename symbolically linked to the old filename.

**truncate** *file, size*

>Truncates *file* to *size*. *file* may be a filename or a filehandle.

**unlink** *list†*

>Deletes a list of files.

**utime** *list*

>Changes the access and modification times. The first two elements of the list must be the numerical access and modification times.

>The inode change time will be set to the current time.

# *Input/Output*

In input/output operations, *filehandle* may be a filehandle as
opened by the open operator, a predefined filehandle (e.g.,
**STDOUT**) or a scalar variable that evaluates to a reference to
or the name of a filehandle to be used.

*<filehandle>*

> In scalar context, reads a single line from the file
> opened on *filehandle*. In list context, reads the rest
> of the file.

*< >*

> Reads from the input stream formed by the files
> specified in **@ARGV**, or standard input if no argu-
> ments were supplied.

binmode *filehandle*

> Arranges for the file opened on *filehandle* to be read
> or written in binary mode as opposed to text mode
> (null operation on Unix or Mac).

close [ *filehandle* ]

> Closes the file or pipe associated with the filehandle.
> Resets $.. If *filehandle* is omitted, closes the cur-
> rently selected filehandle.

dbmclose %*hash*

> Deprecated, use untie instead.

dbmopen %*hash*, *dbmname*, *mode*

> Deprecated, use tie instead.

eof *filehandle*

> Returns true if the next read will return end of file, or
> if the file is not open.

eof

> Returns the EOF status for the last file read.

eof( )

> Indicates EOF on the pseudo-file formed of the files
> listed on the command line.

fcntl *filehandle*, *function*, $*var*

> Implements the *fcntl*(2) function. This function has
> nonstandard return values.

---

**fileno** *filehandle*

> Returns the file descriptor for a given (open) filehandle.

**flock** *filehandle, operation*

> Calls a system-dependent locking routine on the file. *operation* formed by adding 1 (shared), 2 (exclusive), 4 (non-blocking) or 8 (unlock).

**getc** [ *filehandle* ]

> Yields the next character from the file, or an empty string on end of file. If *filehandle* is omitted, reads from **STDIN**.

**ioctl** *filehandle, function, $var*

> Performs *ioctl*(2) on the file. This function has non-standard return values.

**open** *filehandle* [ , *filename* ]

> Opens a file and associates it with *filehandle*. If *filename* is omitted, the scalar variable of the same name as the *filehandle* must contain the filename. The following filename conventions apply when opening a file:
>
> *"file"*    Opens *file* for input. Also *"<file"*.
>
> *">file"*    Opens *file* for output, creating it if necessary.
>
> *">>file"*
>
> > Opens *file* in append mode.
>
> *"+<file"*
>
> > Opens existing *file* with read/write access.
>
> *"+>file"*
>
> > Clobbers old or create new *file* with read/write access.
>
> *"+>>file"*
>
> > Read/write access in append mode.
>
> *"| cmd"*
>
> > Opens a pipe to command *cmd*; forks if *cmd* is -.

---

"*cmd* | "

>Opens a pipe from command *cmd*; forks if *cmd* is -.

*file* may be &*filehnd*, in which case the new file-handle is connected to the (previously opened) filehandle *filehnd*. If it is &=*n*, *file* will be connected to the given file descriptor.

open returns undef upon failure, true otherwise.

pipe *readhandle*, *writehandle*

>Returns a pair of connected pipes.

print [ *filehandle* ] [ *list*† ]

>Prints the elements of *list*, converting them to strings if needed. If *filehandle* is omitted, prints by default to standard output (or to the last selected output channel; see select).

printf [ *filehandle* ] [ *list* ]

>Equivalent to print *filehandle* sprintf *list*.

read *filehandle*, $*var*, *length* [ , *offset* ]

>Reads *length* binary bytes from the file into the variable at *offset*. Returns number of bytes actually read, 0 on eof, and undef on failure.

readline *expr*

>Internal function that implements the < > operator. *expr* must be a typeglob.

readpipe *expr*

>Internal function that implements the qx// operator. *expr* is executed as a system command.

seek *filehandle*, *position*, *whence*

>Arbitrarily positions the file. Returns true if successful.

select [ *filehandle* ]

>Returns the currently selected filehandle. Sets the current default filehandle for output operations if *filehandle* is supplied.

**select** *rbits, wbits, nbits, timeout*

> Performs a *select*(2) system call with the same parameters.

**sprintf** *format, list*

> Returns a string resulting from formatting a (possibly empty) list of values. See the section "Formatted Printing" for a complete list of format conversions. See the section "Formats" for an alternative way to obtain formatted output.

**sysopen** *filehandle, path, mode* [ , *perms* ]

> Performs an *open*(2) system call. The possible values and flag bits of *mode* are system-dependent; they are available via the standard module **Fcntl**.

**sysread** *filehandle, $var, length* [ , *offset* ]

> Reads *length* bytes into $*var* at *offset*. Returns number of bytes actually read, 0 on **eof**, and **undef** on failure.

**sysseek** *filehandle, position, whence*

> Arbitrarily positions the file for use with **sysread** and **syswrite**. See the Perl documentation for details on the nonstandard return values of this function.

**syswrite** *filehandle, scalar, length* [ , *offset* ]

> Writes *length* bytes from *scalar* at *offset*.

**tell** [ *filehandle* ]

> Returns the current file position for the file. If *filehandle* is omitted, assumes the file last read.

## *Formatted Printing*

**printf** and **sprintf** format a list of values according to a format string that may use the following conversions:

| | |
|---|---|
| %% | A percent sign. |
| %c | The character corresponding to the ordinal value. |
| %d | A signed integer. |

| %e | A floating-point number (scientific notation). |
|---|---|
| %f | A floating-point number (fixed decimal notation). |
| %g | A floating-point number (%e or %f notation). |
| %i | A synonym for %d. |
| %n | The number of characters formatted so far is *stored* into the corresponding variable in the parameter list. |
| %o | An unsigned integer, in octal. |
| %p | A pointer (address in hexadecimal). |
| %s | A string. |
| %u | An unsigned integer (decimal). |
| %x | An unsigned integer (hexadecimal). |
| %D | An obsolete synonym for %ld. |
| %E | Like %e, but using an uppercase "E". |
| %F | An obsolete synonym for %f. |
| %G | Like %g, but with an uppercase "E" (if applicable). |
| %O | An obsolete synonym for %lo. |
| %U | An obsolete synonym for %lu. |
| %X | Like %x, but using uppercase letters. |

The following flags can be put between the % and the conversion letter:

| *space* | Prefix a positive number with a space. |
|---|---|
| + | Prefix a positive number with a plus sign. |
| – | Left-justify within the field. |
| 0 | Use zeroes instead of spaces to right-justify. |
| # | Prefix a non-zero octal number with "0", and a non-zero hex number with "0x". |

*number* Minimum field width.

*.number*

> For a floating-point number: the number of digits after the decimal point.
> For a string: the maximum length.
> For an integer: the minimum width.

| l | Interpret integer as "long" or "unsigned long" according to the C type. |
|---|---|
| h | Interpret integer as "short" or "unsigned short" according to the C type. |
| V | Interpret integer according to Perl's type. |

An asterisk (*) may be used instead of a number; the value of the next item in the list will be used.

See the section "Formats" for an alternative way to obtain formatted output.

## *Formats*

formline *picture, list*
> Formats *list* according to *picture* and accumulates the result into $^A.

write [ *filehandle* ]
> Writes a formatted record to the specified file, using the format associated with that file.
> If *filehandle* is omitted, the currently selected one is taken.

Formats are defined as follows:

```
format [ name ] =
formlist
.
```

*formlist* is a sequence of lines, each of which is either a comment line (# in the first column), a picture line, or an argument line.

A picture line contains the arguments which will give values to the fields in the lines. Other text is output as given.

Argument lines contain lists of values that are output in the format and order of the preceding picture line.

*name* defaults to **STDOUT** if omitted.

Picture fields are:

| | |
|---|---|
| @<<<... | Left-adjusted field. Repeat the < to denote the desired width. |
| @>>>... | Right-adjusted field. |
| @\|\|\|... | Centered field. |
| @#.##... | Numeric format with implied decimal point. |
| @* | Multiline field. |

Use ^ instead of @ for multiline block filling.

Use ~ in a picture line to suppress unwanted empty lines.

Use ~~ in a picture line to have this format line repeated until all fields are exhausted.

Set $- to zero to force a page break on the next write.

See also $^, $~, $^A, $^F, $-, and $= in the section "Special Variables."

## Tying Variables

tie *var*, *classname*, [ *list* ]
> Ties a variable to a package class that will handle it. *list* is passed to the class constructor.

tied *var* Returns a reference to the object underlying *var*, or undef if *var* is not tied to a package class.

untie *var*
> Breaks the binding between the variable and the package class.

A class implementing a tied scalar should define the methods **TIESCALAR**, **FETCH**, **STORE**, and possibly **DESTROY**.

A class implementing a tied ordinary array should define the methods **TIEARRAY**, **FETCH**, **STORE**, **FETCHSIZE**, **STORESIZE**, and perhaps **DESTROY**.

A class implementing a tied hash should define the methods **TIEHASH**, **FETCH**, **STORE**, **EXISTS**, **DELETE CLEAR**, **FIRSTKEY**, **NEXTKEY**, and optionally **DESTROY**.

A class implementing a tied filehandle should define the methods **TIEHANDLE**, at least one of **PRINT**, **PRINTF**, **WRITE**, **READLINE**, **GETC**, **READ**, and possibly **CLOSE** and **DESTROY**.

Several base classes to implement tied variables are available in the standard modules library.

## *Directory Reading Routines*

closedir *dirhandle*
> Closes a directory opened by opendir.

opendir *dirhandle*, *dirname*
> Opens a directory on the handle specified.

readdir *dirhandle*
> In scalar context, returns the next entry from the directory or undef if none remains.
> In list context, returns a list of all remaining entries from the directory.

rewinddir *dirhandle*
> Positions the directory to the beginning.

seekdir *dirhandle*, *pos*
> Sets position for readdir on the directory. *pos* should be a file offset as returned by telldir.

telldir *dirhandle*
> Returns the position in the directory.

## *System Interaction*

alarm *expr*
> Schedules a **SIGALRM** to be delivered after *expr* seconds. If *expr* is 0, cancels a pending timer.

**chdir** [ *expr* ]

> Changes the working directory. Uses $ENV{HOME} or $ENV{LOGNAME} if *expr* is omitted.

**chroot** *filename*†

> Changes the root directory for the process and its children.

**die** [ *list* ]

> Prints the value of *list* to **STDERR** and exits with the current value of **$!** (errno). If **$!** is 0, exits with the value of **($? >> 8)**. If **($? >> 8)** is 0, exits with 255. *list* defaults to **"Died"**. Inside an **eval**, the error message is stuffed into **$@**, and the **eval** is terminated and returns **undef**; this makes **die** the way to raise an exception.

**exec** [ *program* ] *list*

> Executes the system command in *list*; does not return. *program* can be used to designate the program to execute *command*.

**exit** [ *expr* ]

> Exits immediately with the value of *expr*, which defaults to 0 (zero). Calls **END** routines and object destructors before exiting.

**fork**

> Does a *fork*(2) system call. Returns the process ID of the child to the parent process (or **undef** on failure) and zero to the child process.

**getlogin**

> Returns the current login name as known by the system. If it returns **false**, use **getpwuid**.

**getpgrp** [ *pid* ]

> Returns the process group for process *pid* (0, or omitted, means the current process).

**getppid**

> Returns the process ID of the parent process.

**getpriority** *which*, *who*

> Returns the current priority for a process, process group, or user. Use **getpriority 0,0** to designate the current process.

glob *pat*   Returns a list of filenames that match the shell pattern *pat*.

kill *list*   Sends a signal to a list of processes. The first element of the list must be the signal to send (either numeric, or its name as a string). Negative signals kill process groups instead of processes.

setpgrp *pid, pgrp*
  Sets the process group for the *pid* (0 means the current process).

setpriority *which, who, priority*
  Sets the current priority for a process, process group, or a user.

sleep [ *expr* ]
  Causes the program to sleep for *expr* seconds, or forever if no *expr*. Returns the number of seconds actually slept.

syscall *list*
  Calls the system call specified in the first element of the list, passing the rest of the list as arguments to the call. Returns −1 on error.

system [ *program* ] *list*
  Does exactly the same thing as **exec** *list* except that a fork is performed first, and the parent process waits for the child process to complete. During the wait, the signals **SIGINT** and **SIGQUIT** are passed to the child process.

  Returns the exit status of the child process. 0 indicates success, not failure.

  *program* can be used to designate the program to execute *command*.

times   Returns a 4-element list (0:$user, 1:$system, 2:$cuser, 3:$csystem) giving the user and system times, in seconds, for this process and the children of this process.

**umask** [ *expr* ]

> Sets the umask for the process and returns the old one. If *expr* is omitted, returns current umask value.

**wait**

> Waits for a child process to terminate and returns the process ID of the deceased process (–1 if none). The status is returned in **$?**.

**waitpid** *pid, flags*

> Performs the same function as the corresponding system call. Returns 1 when process *pid* is dead, –1 if nonexistent.

**warn** [ *list* ]

> Prints *list* on **STDERR** like die, but doesn't exit. *list* defaults to **"Warning: something's wrong"**.

## Networking

**accept** *newsocket, genericsocket*

> Accepts a new socket.

**bind** *socket, name*

> Binds the *name* to the *socket*.

**connect** *socket, name*

> Connects the *name* to the *socket*.

**getpeername** *socket*

> Returns the socket address of the other end of the *socket*.

**getsockname** *socket*

> Returns the name of the socket.

**getsockopt** *socket, level, optname*

> Returns the socket options.

**listen** *socket, queuesize*

> Starts listening on the specified *socket*, allowing *queuesize* connections.

**recv** *socket, $var, length, flags*

> Receives a message on *socket* of *length* bytes into scalar variable **$var**.

send *socket, msg, flags* [ , *to* ]
> Sends a message on the *socket*.

setsockopt *socket, level, optname, optval*
> Sets the requested socket option.

shutdown *socket, how*
> Shuts down a *socket*.

socket *socket, domain, type, protocol*
> Creates a *socket* in *domain* with *type* and *protocol*.

socketpair *socket1, socket2, domain, type, protocol*
> Works the same as socket, but creates a pair of bidirectional sockets.

## *System V IPC*

Depending on your system configuration, certain system files need to be required to access the message- and semaphore-specific operation names.

msgctl *id, cmd, args*
> Calls *msgctl*(2). If *cmd* is **&IPC_STAT** then *args* must be a variable. See the Perl documentation for details on the nonstandard return values of this function.

msgget *key, flags*
> Creates a message queue for *key*. Returns the message queue identifier.

msgrcv *id, $var, size, type, flags*
> Receives a message from queue *id* into $*var*.

msgsnd *id, msg, flags*
> Sends *msg* to queue *id*.

semctl *id, semnum, cmd, arg*
> Calls *semctl*(2). If *cmd* is **&IPC_STAT** or **&GETALL** then *arg* must be a variable.

semget *key, nsems, size, flags*
> Creates a set of semaphores for *key*. Returns the message semaphore identifier.

**semop** *key*, ...

> Performs semaphore operations.

**shmctl** *id*, *cmd*, *arg*

> Calls *shmctl*(2). If *cmd* is **&IPC_STAT** then *arg* must be a scalar variable.

**shmget** *key*, *size*, *flags*

> Creates shared memory. Returns the shared memory segment identifier.

**shmread** *id*, $*var*, *pos*, *size*

> Reads at most *size* bytes of the contents of shared memory segment *id* starting at offset *pos* into $*var*.

**shmwrite** *id*, *string*, *pos*, *size*

> Writes at most *size* bytes of *string* into the contents of shared memory segment *id* at offset *pos*.

## Miscellaneous

**defined** *expr*

> Tests whether the *expr* has an actual value.

**do** *filename*

> Executes *filename* as a Perl script. See also **require** in the section "Subroutines, Packages, and Modules."

**dump** [ *label* ]

> Immediate core dump. When reincarnated, starts at *label*. Obsolete.

**eval** { *expr*, ... }

> Executes the code between { and }. Traps runtime errors and returns as described with **eval**(*expr*), in the section "String Functions."

**local** *variable*

> Gives a temporary value to the named package variable, which lasts until the enclosing block, file, or **eval** exits.

**my** *variable*

> Creates a scope for the variable lexically local to the
> enclosing block, file, or **eval**.

**ref** *expr*†

> Returns a **true** value if *expr* is a reference. Returns
> the package name if *expr* has been blessed into a
> package.

**reset** [ *expr* ]

> *expr* is a string of single letters. All variables begin-
> ning with one of those letters are reset to their pris-
> tine state.
>
> If *expr* is omitted, resets ?? searches so that they
> work again.
>
> Only affects the current package.

**undef** *lvalue*†

> Undefines the *lvalue*. Always returns the undefined
> value.

# *Information from System Databases*

## *Information About Users*

In scalar context, each of these routines returns a 10-element
list: (0:$name, 1:$passwd, 2:$uid, 3:$gid, 4:$quota, 5:$com-
ment, 6:$gcos, 7:$dir, 8:$shell, 9:$expire).

Use the standard module **User::pwent** for easy access to this
information.

**endpwent**

> Ends lookup processing.

**getpwent**

> Gets next user information.
> In scalar context, returns the username.

**getpwnam** *name*

> Gets information by name.
> In scalar context, returns the user ID.

---

getpwuid *uid*

        Gets information by user ID.

        In scalar context, returns the username.

setpwent

        Resets lookup processing.

## *Information About Groups*

In list context, each of these routines returns a 4-element list: (0:$name, 1:$passwd, 2:$gid, 3:$members).

$members contains a space-separated list of the login names of the group members.

Use the standard module **User::grent** for easy access to this information.

endgrent

        Ends lookup processing.

getgrent   Gets next group information.

        In scalar context, returns the group name.

getgrgid *gid*

        Gets information by group ID.

        In scalar context, returns the group name.

getgrnam *name*

        Gets information by name.

        In scalar context, returns the group ID.

setgrent   Resets lookup processing.

## *Information About Networks*

In list context, each of these routines returns a 4-element list: (0:$name, 1:$aliases, 2:$addrtype, 3:$net).

Use the standard module **Net::netent** for easy access to this information.

endnetent

        Ends lookup processing.

getnetbyaddr *addr*, *type*

        Gets information by address and type.

        In scalar context, returns the network name.

**getnetbyname** *name*

        Gets information by network name.

        In scalar context, returns the network number.

**getnetent**

        Gets next network information.

        In scalar context, returns the network name.

**setnetent** *stayopen*

        Resets lookup processing.

## *Information About Network Hosts*

In list context, each of these routines returns a list of at least
5 elements: (0:$name, 1:$aliases, 2:$addrtype, 3:$length,
4:$addr [ , more addresses ] ).

Use the standard module **Net::hostent** for easy access to this
information.

**endhostent**

        Ends lookup processing.

**gethostbyaddr** *addr, addrtype*

        Gets information by IP address.

        In scalar context, returns the hostname.

**gethostbyname** *name*

        Gets information by hostname.

        In scalar context, returns the host address.

**gethostent**

        Gets next host information.

        In scalar context, returns the hostname.

**sethostent** *stayopen*

        Resets lookup processing.

## *Information About Network Services*

In list context, each of these routines returns a 4-element list:
(0:$name, 1:$aliases, 2:$port, 3:$proto).

Use the standard module **Net::servent** for easy access to this
information.

endserver

> Ends lookup processing.

getservbyname *name, proto*

> Gets information by service name.
> In scalar context, returns the port number.

getservbyport *port, proto*

> Gets information by service port.
> In scalar context, returns the service name.

getservent

> Gets next service information.
> In scalar context, returns the service name.

setservent *stayopen*

> Resets lookup processing.

## *Information About Network Protocols*

In list context, each of these routines returns a 3-element list:
(0:$name, 1:$aliases, 2:$proto).

Use the standard module **Net::protoent** for easy access to this
information.

endprotoent

> Ends lookup processing.

getprotobyname *name*

> Gets information by protocol name.
> In scalar context, returns the protocol number.

getprotobynumber *number*

> Gets information by protocol number.
> In scalar context, returns the protocol name.

getprotoent

> Gets next protocol information.
> In scalar context, returns the protocol name.

setprotoent *stayopen*

> Resets lookup processing.

## Special Variables

The alternative names are provided by the standard module **English**.

The following variables are global and should be localized in subroutines:

**$_**   Alternative: $ARG.
         The default input, output, and pattern-searching space.

**$.**   Alternative: $INPUT_LINE_NUMBER, $NR.
         The current input line number of the last filehandle read.

**$/**   Alternative: $INPUT_RECORD_SEPARATOR, $RS.
         The input record separator, newline by default. May be multicharacter.

**$,**   Alternative: $OUTPUT_FIELD_SEPARATOR, $OFS.
         The output field separator for the print function.

**$"**   Alternative: $LIST_SEPARATOR.
         The separator that joins elements of arrays interpolated in strings.

**$\**   Alternative: $OUTPUT_RECORD_SEPARATOR, $ORS.
         The output record separator for the print function.

**$#**   The output format for printed numbers. Deprecated. Use printf instead.

**$***   Set to 1 to do multiline matching within strings. Deprecated; see the m and s modifiers in the section "Search and Replace Functions."

**$?**   Alternative: $CHILD_ERROR.
         The status returned by the last `...` command, pipe close, wait, waitpid, or system function.

**$]**   Alternative: $PERL_VERSION.
         The Perl version number, e.g., 5.005.

| | |
|---|---|
| $[ | The index of the first element in an array or list, and of the first character in a substring. Default is 0. Deprecated. Do not use. |
| $; | Alternative: $SUBSCRIPT_SEPARATOR, $SUBSEP. The subscript separator for multidimensional list emulation. Default is "\034". |
| $! | Alternative: $OS_ERROR, $ERRNO. Used in a numeric context, yields the current value of errno. Used in a string context, yields the corresponding error string. |
| $@ | Alternative: $EVAL_ERROR. The Perl error message from the last eval or do *expr* command. |
| $: | Alternative: $FORMAT_LINE_BREAK_CHARACTERS. The set of characters after which a string may be broken to fill continuation fields (starting with ^) in a format. |
| $0 | Alternative: $PROGRAM_NAME. The name of the file containing the Perl script being executed. May be assigned to. |
| $$ | Alternative: $PROCESS_ID, $PID. The process ID of the Perl interpreter running this script. Altered (in the child process) by fork. |
| $< | Alternative: $REAL_USER_ID, $UID. The real user ID of this process. |
| $> | Alternative: $EFFECTIVE_USER_ID, $EUID. The effective user ID of this process. |
| $( | Alternative: $REAL_GROUP_ID, $GID. The real group ID, or space-separated list of group IDs, of this process. |
| $) | Alternative: $EFFECTIVE_GROUP_ID, $EGID. The effective group ID, or space-separated list of group IDs, of this process. |
| $^A | Alternative: $ACCUMULATOR. The accumulator for formline and write operations. |

| $^D | Alternative: $DEBUGGING. |
| | The debug flags as passed to Perl using -D. |
| $^E | Alternative: $EXTENDED_OS_ERROR. |
| | Operating system dependent error information. |
| $^F | Alternative: $SYSTEM_FD_MAX. |
| | The highest system file descriptor, ordinarily 2. |
| $^H | The current state of syntax checks. |
| $^I | Alternative: $INPLACE_EDIT. |
| | In-place edit extension as passed to Perl using -i. |
| $^L | Alternative: $FORMAT_FORMFEED. |
| | Formfeed character used in formats. |
| $^M | Emergency memory pool. |
| $^O | Alternative: $OSNAME. |
| | Operating system name. |
| $^P | Alternative: $PERLDB. |
| | Internal debugging flag. |
| $^S | Current state of the Perl interpreter. |
| $^T | Alternative: $BASETIME. |
| | The time (as delivered by time) when the program |
| | started. This value is used by the file test operators |
| | -M, -A, and -C. |
| $^W | Alternative: $WARNING. |
| | The value of the -w option as passed to Perl. |
| $^X | Alternative: $EXECUTABLE_NAME. |
| | The name by which this Perl interpreter was |
| | invoked. |

The following variables are context dependent and need not
be localized:

| $% | Alternative: $FORMAT_PAGE_NUMBER. |
| | The current page number of the currently selected |
| | output channel. |
| $= | Alternative: $FORMAT_LINES_PER_PAGE. |
| | The page length of the current output channel. |
| | Default is 60 lines. |

---

| $-     | Alternative: $FORMAT_LINES_LEFT. |
|        | The number of lines remaining on the page. |
| $~     | Alternative: $FORMAT_NAME. |
|        | The name of the current report format. |
| $^     | Alternative: $FORMAT_TOP_NAME. |
|        | The name of the current top-of-page format. |
| $\|    | Alternative: $OUTPUT_AUTOFLUSH. |
|        | If set to nonzero, forces a flush after every write or print on the currently selected output channel. Default is 0. |

**$ARGV**  The name of the current file when reading from < >.

The following variables are always local to the current block:

| $&     | Alternative: $MATCH. |
|        | The string matched by the last successful pattern match. |
| $`     | Alternative: $PREMATCH. |
|        | The string preceding what was matched by the last successful match. |
| $'     | Alternative: $POSTMATCH. |
|        | The string following what was matched by the last successful match. |
| $+     | Alternative: $LAST_PAREN_MATCH. |
|        | The last bracket matched by the last search pattern. |

**$1...$9...**

Contain the subpatterns from the corresponding sets of parentheses in the last pattern successfully matched. $10 and up are only available if the match contained that many subpatterns.

# Special Arrays

The alternative names are provided by the standard module **English**.

**@ARGV**  Contains the command-line arguments for the script (not including the command name, which is in **$0**).

**@EXPORT**

  Names the methods and other symbols a package exports by default.

**@EXPORT_OK**

  Names the methods and other symbols a package can export upon explicit request.

**@F**  When command-line option **-a** is used, contains the split of the input lines.

**@INC**  Contains the list of places to look for Perl scripts to be evaluated by the **do** *filename*, **use** and **require** commands. Do not modify directly, but use the **use lib** pragma or **-I** command-line option instead.

**@ISA**  List of base classes of the current package.

**@_**  Alternative: @ARG.
  Parameter array for subroutines. Also used by **split** if not in list context.

# Special Hashes

**%ENV**  Contains the current environment. The key is the name of an environment variable; the value is its current setting.

**%EXPORT_TAGS**

  Defines names for sets of symbols.

**%INC**  List of files that have been included with **use**, **require**, or **do**. The key is the filename as specified; the value the location of the file.

---

**%SIG**     Used to set signal handlers for various signals. The key is the name of the signal (without the **SIG** prefix); the value a subroutine that is executed when the signal occurs.

__WARN__ and __DIE__ are pseudo-signals to attach handlers to Perl warnings and exceptions.

## Standard Modules

**AnyDBM_File**
    Provides a framework for multiple dbm files.

**AutoLoader**
    Loads functions only on demand.

**AutoSplit**
    Splits a package for autoloading.

**B**     Experimental package that implements byte compilation, a Perl to C translator, and other interesting things.

**Benchmark**
    Benchmarks running times of code.

**Bundle::CPAN**
    A bundle to play with all the other modules on CPAN.

**Carp**     Warns of errors.

**CGI**     Simple Common Gateway Interface Class.

**CGI::Apache**
    CGI addition for Apache's Perl API.

**CGI::Cookie**
    Interface to Netscape Cookies.

**CGI:Fast**
    CGI interface for FastCGI.

**CGI:Push**
    Simple interface to Server Push.

**Class::Struct**

    Declares struct-like datatypes as Perl classes.

**Config**    Accesses Perl configuration information.

**CPAN**    Maintenance of Perl modules from CPAN sites.

**Cwd**    Gets the pathname of the current working directory.

**Data::Dumper**

    Reveals Perl data structures as strings.

**DB_File**    Access to Berkeley DB files.

**Devel::SelfStubber**

    Generates stubs for a SelfLoading module.

**Dirhandle**

    Supplies object methods for directory handles.

**DynaLoader**

    Dynamically loads C libraries into Perl code.

**English**    Uses nice English names for ugly punctuation variables.

**Env**    Imports environment variables.

**Exporter**

    Implements default import method for modules.

**ExtUtils::Command**

    Replacements for common Unix commands (for Makefiles).

**ExtUtils::Embed**

    Utilities for embedding Perl in C/C++ applications.

**ExtUtils::Install**

    Installs files from here to there.

**ExtUtils::Installed**

    Inventory management of installed modules.

**ExtUtils::Liblist**

    Determines libraries to use and how to use them.

**ExtUtils::MakeMaker**

    Creates an extension Makefile.

**ExtUtils::Manifest**

Utilities to write and check a MANIFEST file.

**ExtUtils::Miniperl**

Writes the C code for **perlmain.c**.

**ExtUtils::Mkbootstrap**

Makes a bootstrap file for use by DynaLoader.

**ExtUtils::Mksymlists**

Writes linker options files for dynamic extension.

**ExtUtils::MM_OS2**

Methods to override Unix behavior in
ExtUtils::MakeMaker.

**ExtUtils::MM_Unix**

Methods used by ExtUtils::MakeMaker.

**ExtUtils::MM_VMS**

Methods to override Unix behavior in
ExtUtils::MakeMaker.

**ExtUtils::MM_Win32**

Methods to override Unix behavior in
ExtUtils::MakeMaker.

**ExtUtils::Packlist**

Manages _.packlist_ files.

**ExtUtils::testlib**

Adds blib directories to @INC.

**Fatal**    Replaces functions with equivalents that succeed or
die.

**Fcntl**    Loads the C **fcntl.h** defines.

**File::Basename**

Parses file specifications.

**File::CheckTree**

Runs many filetest checks on a tree.

**File::Copy**

Copies files or filehandles.

**File::DosGlob**

DOS-like globbing (with extensions).

---

**File::Find**

> Traverses a file tree.

**File::Path**

> Creates or remove a series of directories.

**File::Spec**

> Portably performs operations on filenames.

**File::Spec::Mac**

> Methods for MacOS file specs.

**File::Spec::OS2**

> Methods for OS/2 file specs.

**File::Spec::Unix**

> Methods used by File::Spec for Unix.

**File::Spec::VMS**

> Methods for VMS file specs.

**File::Spec::Win32**

> Methods for Win32 file specs.

**File::stat**

> By name interface to Perl's built-in stat functions.

**FileCache**

> Keeps more files open than the system permits.

**FileHandle**

> Supplies object methods for filehandles.

**FindBin** Locates directory of original Perl script.

**GDBM_File**

> Access to the gdbm library.

**Getopt::Long**

> Extended handling of command-line options. Suits all needs.

**Getopt::Std**

> Processes single-character switches with switch clustering.

**I18N::Collate**

> Compares 8-bit scalar data according to the current locale.

---

**IO**  Loads various I/O modules.

**IO::File**  Supplies object methods for filehandles.

**IO::Handle**
Supplies object methods for I/O handles.

**IO::Pipe**
Supplies object methods for pipes.

**IO::Seekable**
Supplies seek-based methods for I/O objects.

**IO::Select**
Object interface to the select system call.

**IO::Socket**
Object interface to socket communications.

**IPC::Msg**
Interface to System V Message IPC.

**IPC::Open2**
Open a pipe to a process for both reading and writing.

**IPC::Open3**
Open a pipe to a process for reading, writing, and error handling.

**IPC::Semaphore**
Interface to System V semaphores.

**IPC::SysV**
System V IPC object class.

**Math::BigFloat**
Arbitrary length float math package.

**Math::BigInt**
Arbitrary size integer math package.

**Math::Complex**
Complex numbers and associated mathematical functions.

**NDBM_File**
tied access to ndbm files.

---

**Net::hostent**

>Access by name to gethostent and friends.

**Net::netent**

>Access by name to getnetent and friends.

**Net::Ping**

>Checks whether a host is up.

**Net::protoent**

>Access by name to getprotoent and friends.

**Net::servent**

>Access by name to getservent and friends.

**O**          Experimental compiler backend.

**Opcode**     Disables named opcodes when compiling Perl code.

**OS2::ExtAttr**

>Perl access to extended attributes. OS/2 only.

**OS2::PrfDB**

>Perl extension to access the OS/2 setting database.
>OS/2 only.

**OS2::Process**

>Constants for system() call on OS/2. OS/2 only.

**OS2::REXX**

>Access to DLLs with REXX calling convention and
>REXX runtime. OS/2 only.

**Pod::Html**

>Module to convert POD files to HTML.

**Pod::Text**

>Converts POD data to formatted ASCII text.

**POSIX**      Interface to IEEE Std 1003.1.

**Safe**       Compiles and executes code in restricted
>compartments.

**SDBM_File**

>tied access to sdbm files.

**Search::Dict**

>Searches for key in dictionary file.

---

**SelectSaver**
Saves and restores a selected filehandle.

**SelfLoader**
Loads functions only on demand.

**Shell** Runs shell commands transparently within Perl.

**Socket** Loads the C **socket.h** defines and structure manipulators.

**Symbol** Manipulates Perl symbols and their names.

**Sys::Hostname**
Tries every conceivable way to get the name of this system.

**Sys::Syslog**
Interface to the Unix *syslog*(3) calls.

**Term::Cap**
Perl interface to Unix *termcap*(3).

**Term::Complete**
Word completion module.

**Term::ReadLine**
Interface to various readline packages.

**Test::Harness**
Runs Perl standard test scripts with statistics.

**Text::Abbrev**
Creates an abbreviation table from a list.

**Text::ParseWords**
Parses text into a list of tokens.

**Text::Soundex**
Implementation of the Soundex Algorithm as described by Donald Knuth.

**Text::Tabs**
Expands and unexpands tabs.

**Text::Wrap**
Line wrapping to form simple paragraphs.

**Thread** Implementation of Perl threads.

---

**Thread::Queue**
    Implementation of thread-safe queues.
**Thread::Semaphore**
    Implementation of thread-safe semaphores.
**Thread::Signal**
    Implementation of reliable signals using threads.
**Thread::Specific**
    Thread-specific keys.
**Tie::Arrays**
    Base class definitions for tied arrays.
**Tie::Handle**
    Base class definitions for tied filehandles.
**Tie::Hash**
    Base class definitions for tied hashes.
**Tie::RefHash**
    Use references as hash keys.
**Tie::Scalar**
    Base class definitions for tied scalars.
**Tie::StdHash**
    Basic methods for tied hashes.
**Tie::StdScalar**
    Basic methods for tied scalars.
**Tie::SubstrHash**
    Fixed table-size, fixed key-length hashing.
**Time::Local**
    Efficiently computes time from local and GMT time.
**UNIVERSAL**
    Base class for all classes (blessed references).
**User::grent**
    Access by name to getgrent and friends.
**User::pwent**
    Access by name to getpwent and friends.

**VMS::DCLsym**

> Perl extension to manipulate DCL symbols. VMS only.

**VMS::Filespec**

> Converts between VMS and Unix file specification syntax. VMS only.

**VMS::Stdio**

> Standard I/O functions via VMS extensions. VMS only.

**VMS::XSSymSet**

> Keeps sets of symbol names palatable to the VMS linker.

## Environment Variables

Perl uses the following environment variables:

**HOME**   Used if chdir has no argument.

**LOGDIR**

> Used if chdir has no argument and **HOME** is not set.

**PATH**   Used in executing subprocesses, and in finding the Perl script if -S is used.

**PERL5LIB**

> A colon-separated list of directories to look in for Perl library files before looking in the standard library and the current directory.

**PERL5DB**

> The command to get the debugger code. Defaults to **BEGIN { require 'perl5db.pl' }**.

**PERLLIB**

> Used instead of **PERL5LIB** if the latter is not defined.

# Multithreading

*Multithreading is an experimental feature in this release. Support for multithreading needs to be built into the Perl executable.*

Multithreading requires the standard module **Thread**. This module implements the join, detach, and yield methods discussed here:

**$*thr* -> detach**

> Detach a thread so it runs independently.

[ **$*result* =** ] **$*thr* -> join**

> Wait for the thread to complete. The value returned is the return value from the thread's subroutine.

lock *variable*

> Lock a resource against concurrent access.

**$*thr* = new Thread** *sub* [ *args* ]

> Creates a new thread that starts executing in the referenced subroutine. The *args* are passed to this subroutine.
>
> The return value of this subroutine is delivered by the join method.

yield    Explicitly give up the CPU to some other thread.

# The Perl Compiler

*The Perl Compiler is an experimental feature in this release.*

To compile a Perl program **foo.pl** with the C backend:
    **perl -MO=C,-ofoo.c foo.pl**

To compile **foo.pl** with the CC backend:
    **perl -MO=CC,-ofoo.c foo.pl**

Walk the opcode tree in execution order, printing terse information about each opcode:
    **perl -MO=Terse,exec foo.pl**

Walk the opcode tree in syntax order, printing lengthier debug information about each opcode:

**perl –MO=Debug foo.pl**

You can also append ",**exec**" to walk in execution order.

Produce a cross-reference report of the line numbers at which all variables, subroutines, and formats are defined and used:

**perl –MO=Xref foo.pl**

## *The Perl Debugger*

The Perl symbolic debugger is invoked with **perl –d**.

**a** [ *line* ] *command*

Sets an action for *line*.

**A**  Deletes all line actions.

**b** [ *line* [ *condition* ]]

Sets breakpoint at *line*; default is the current line.

**b** *sub* [ *condition* ]

Sets breakpoint at the named subroutine.

**b compile** *subname*

Stop after the subroutine is compiled.

**b load** *file*

Sets breakpoint at requireing the given file.

**b postpone** *subname* [ *condition* ]

Sets breakpoint at the first line of the subroutine after it is compiled.

**c** [ *line* ]

Continues (until *line*, or another breakpoint, or exit).

**d** [ *line* ]

Deletes breakpoint at the given *line*; default is the current line.

**D**  Deletes all breakpoints.

**f** *file*  Switches to *file* and starts listing it.

**h**  Prints out a long help message.

**h** *cmd*   Prints out help for the command *cmd*.

**h h**      Prints out a concise help message.

**H** [ *−number* ]

     Displays the last *−number* commands.

**l** [ *range* ]

     Lists a range of lines. *range* may be a number, start–end, start+amount, or a subroutine name. If *range* is omitted, lists next window.

**l** *sub*   Lists the named subroutine.

**L**       Lists lines that have breakpoints or actions.

**m** *class*  Prints the methods callable via the given *class*.

**m** *expr*  Evaluates the expression in list context, prints the methods callable on the first element of the result.

**n** [ *expr* ]

     Single steps around the subroutine call.

**O** [ *opt* [ = *val* ] ]

     Sets or queries values of debugger options.

**p** *expr*  Prints *expr*.

**q**       Quits. You may also use your EOF character.

**r**       Returns from the current subroutine.

**R**      Restarts the debugger.

**s** [ *expr* ]

     Single steps.

**S** [ **!** ] *pattern*

     Lists the names of all subroutines [not] matching the pattern.

**t**       Toggles trace mode.

**t** *expr*  Traces through execution of *expr*.

**T**      Prints a stack trace.

**V** [ *package* [ *pattern* ] ]

     Lists variables matching *pattern* in a *package*. Default package is **main**.

---

**w** [ *line* ]
> Lists window around the specified line.

**W**      Deletes all watch-expressions.

**W** *expr*   Adds a global watch-expression.

**x** *expr*   Evaluates *expr* in list context, dumps the result.

**X** [ *pattern* ]
> Like **V**, but assumes current package.

*command*
> Executes *command* as a Perl statement.

.       Returns to the executed line.

–       Lists previous window.

**=** [ *alias value* ]
> Sets alias, or lists current aliases.

*/pattern/*
> Searches forward for *pattern*.

*?pattern?*
> Searches backward for *pattern*.

**<** *command*
> Sets an action to be executed before every debugger
> prompt.

**<<** *command*
> Adds an action to the list of actions to be executed
> before every debugger prompt.

**>** *command*
> Sets an action to be executed after every debugger
> prompt.

**>>** *command*
> Adds an action to the list of actions to be executed
> after every debugger prompt.

**{** *cmd*   Defines a debugger command to run before each
> prompt.

**{{** *cmd*   Adds a debugger command to the list of debugger
> commands to run before each prompt.

! [ [ - ] *number* ]

> Re-executes a command. Default is the previous command.

! [ *pattern* ]

> Re-executes the last command that started with *pattern*.

!! [ *command* ]

> Runs *command* in a subprocess.

| *cmd*  Run debugger command *cmd* through the current pager.

|| *cmd*  Same, temporarily selects **DB::OUT** as well.

RETURN  Repeats last **s** or **n**.